Presented to

From

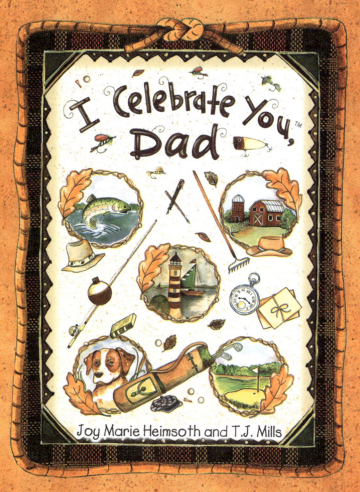

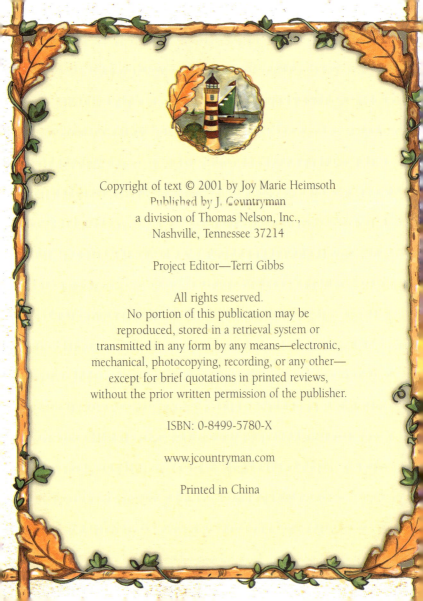

Copyright of text © 2001 by Joy Marie Heimsoth
Published by J. Countryman
a division of Thomas Nelson, Inc.,
Nashville, Tennessee 37214

Project Editor—Terri Gibbs

All rights reserved.
No portion of this publication may be
reproduced, stored in a retrieval system or
transmitted in any form by any means—electronic,
mechanical, photocopying, recording, or any other—
except for brief quotations in printed reviews,
without the prior written permission of the publisher.

ISBN: 0-8499-5780-X

www.jcountryman.com

Printed in China

Dad—
jack-of-all-trades,
counselor and friend,
storyteller, comforter,
giant among
men.

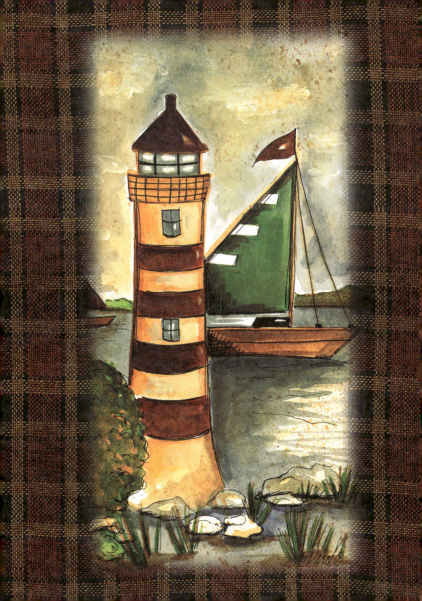

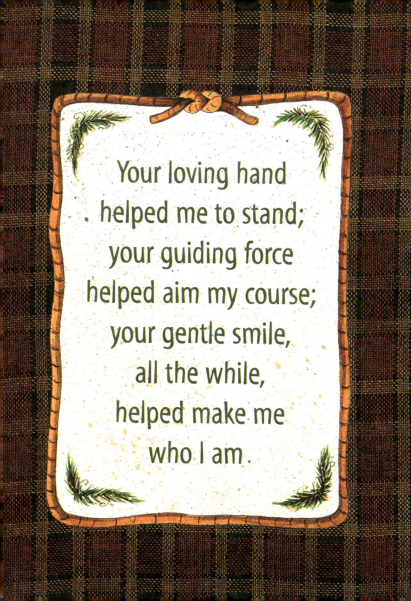

Your loving hand
helped me to stand;
your guiding force
helped aim my course;
your gentle smile,
all the while,
helped make me
who I am.

I Celebrate You

One of the things I appreciate most about you, Dad, is…

_____
_____
_____
_____
_____
_____
_____
_____

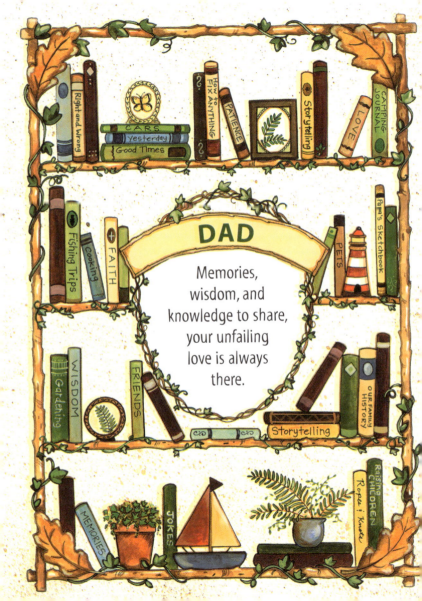

Eyes of understanding,
heart of patience
and love,
hands of comfort
and compassion,
blessed by God above.
I love you
Dad!

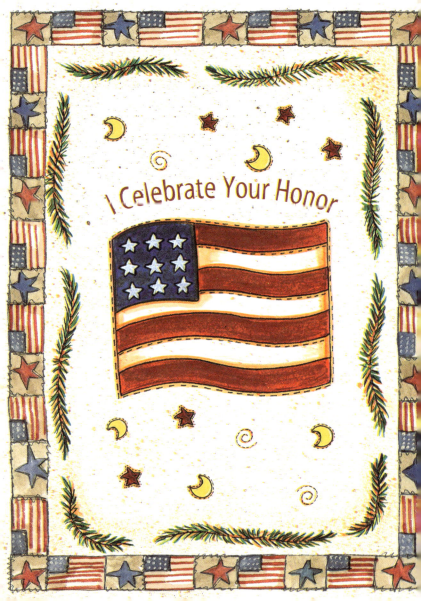

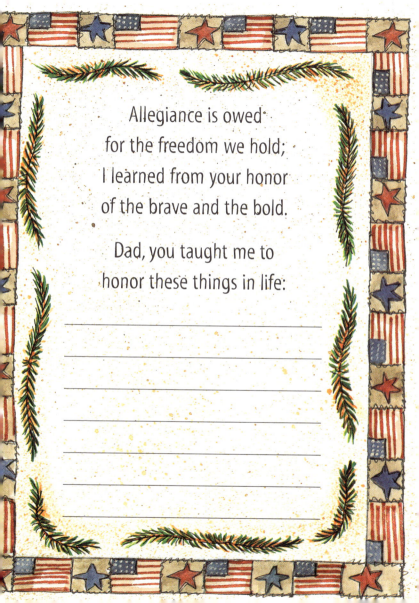

Allegiance is owed
for the freedom we hold;
I learned from your honor
of the brave and the bold.

Dad, you taught me to
honor these things in life:

_____
_____
_____
_____
_____
_____
_____

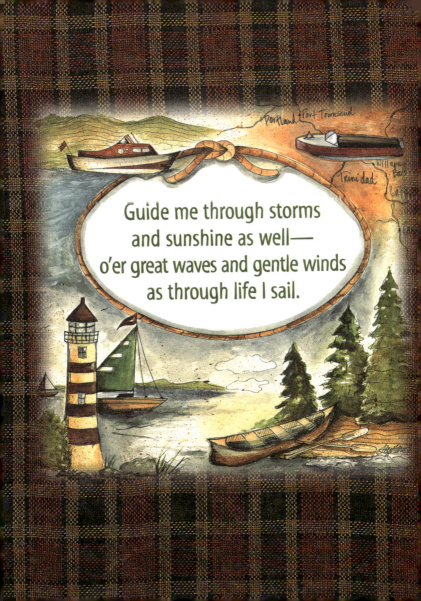

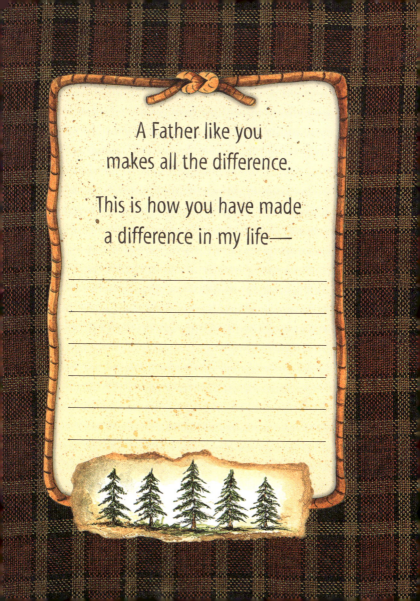

A Father like you
makes all the difference.

This is how you have made
a difference in my life—

These are some of the things I enjoy doing with you—

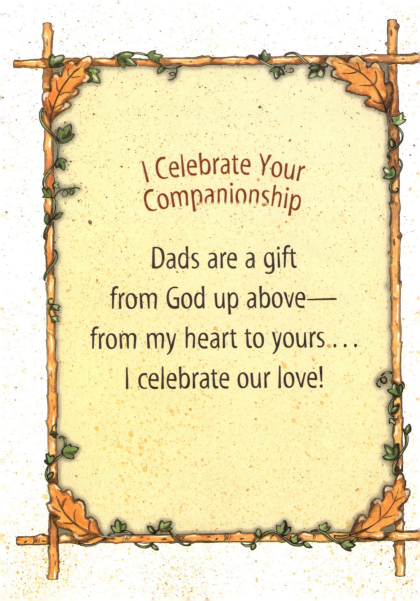

I Celebrate Your Companionship

Dads are a gift
from God up above—
from my heart to yours…
I celebrate our love!

A Father holds
your hand for awhile,
your spirit while he can,
and your heart forever.

This is my prayer for you, Dad—

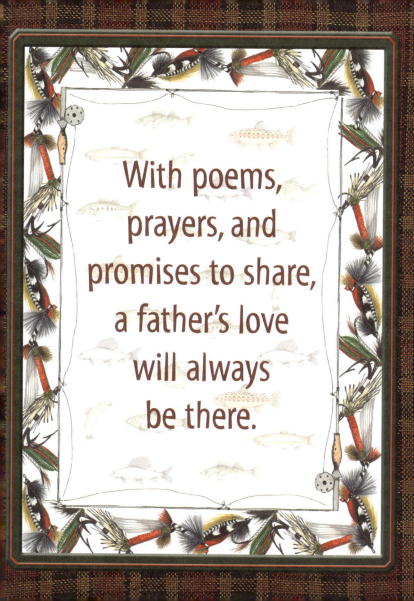

For all the sad
you turned to glad,
for all the care
you gave in prayer,
for all the gold
my heart now holds—

I Celebrate You Dad!